THE ECHO

A CALL TO GREATNESS

SHERRI BROOKS

Copyright © 2024 by Sherri Brooks

All rights reserved.

For Kennen Brooks:

You have been my supporter, biggest cheerleader, encourager, protector, and confidante. You have challenged me to never settle but to let my personal greatness shine. Thank you for your genuine love and devotion. It is my honor and privilege to walk by your side as your wife, lover, and friend.

Contents

	The E.C.H.O.	7
1.	The Power Ps	13
2.	**E**xcellence	43
3.	**C**onsistency	53
4.	**H**ustle	61
5.	**O**pportunity	69
6.	Pivotal People	77
7.	Your Life's Blueprint	91
	Final Thoughts	97
	Notes	103
	About the Author	105

Introduction

The E.C.H.O.

There is a call to greatness in each of us. Its fulfillment lies in our ability to perceive and respond to the summons.

History has seen its share of people who we call "great" based on their discoveries, talents, and even those that have gone against the social structures of their time. They are called great because of their accomplishments and contributions to science, medicine, the arts, and other areas of life. Today, this person is often called the "GOAT", or the Greatest of All Time for their respective forums. For instance, during the 2024 Summer Olympics in Paris, France, gymnast Simone Biles cemented her claim as the "GOAT" in women's gymnastics. She currently holds 30 World Championship and 10 Olympic medals, making her the most decorated gymnast in history. During the 2024 Olympics, she won her second women's individual all-around gold medal, becoming only the third woman in the world to accomplish this feat twice. She broke a 120-year-old record to become the only U.S. gymnast to win seven Olympic gold medals. In her more than 10 years of dominance in the sport, she has redefined women's gymnastics with five signature skills named for her. What also makes her great is that she transcends her sport with her openness about her struggles with mental health issues.

While we typically think of the term GOAT as it relates to sports, the truth is we all want to be great at something. We have an inherent need to achieve success in just about any area of life you can think of, from love, to work, to raising a family. At its core, greatness is not about being famous, fortunate, or fearless. Greatness is not defined by the discovery of some earth-shattering scientific breakthrough or new social media app nor by culture, your income, athletic prowess, or your number of "likes" on Facebook.

Within each of us, there is an inner voice of greatness living deep within our being. This inner voice is the repeating intuition and feeling that there is more, something significant, something important you are to do or become. It is compelling us to be more than we are currently. It is the voice of our Maker who designed us for accomplishment, created us for success, and gifted us with the ability for greatness.

While this is not a book on faith or religion, I believe that when you live beneath the Creator's will and purpose for your life, you intuitively know something is missing. You may have a sense of longing or find yourself on a quest to discover the meaning of life. I propose that what you are experiencing is the resounding of your potential, purpose, and personal calling, lying unrealized, beckoning you to hear and give it attention. It is the *ECHO – A Call to Greatness.*

In this book, I will provide you with what I consider to be the keys it takes to unlock your personal greatness. These keys are a set of qualities and habits anyone can learn and adopt to get to the 'great' in your life. While no two greats look alike, everyone can achieve their God given greatness by leaning into the compelling voice of the ECHO.

As you read this book, I ask that you embrace your journey and know it may not always be straightforward. I believe that if you open yourself to possibilities, be fully present in the moments of your life, and learn to adapt to your circumstances, you *can* achieve greatness. I encourage you to take time to reflect on and write your responses to the questions within some chapters to help you discover the areas you need to lean into.

Let's get started!

> BE NOT AFRAID OF GREATNESS. SOME ARE BORN GREAT, SOME ACHIEVE GREATNESS, AND OTHERS HAVE GREATNESS THRUST UPON THEM.
>
> William Shakespeare

Chapter 1

The Power Ps

"To live is to choose. But to choose well, you must know who you are and what you stand for, where you want to go and why you want to get there."

- Kofi Annan

There are those who dream of greatness and those who achieve greatness. The difference lies in knowing which of these you are. Are you a dreamer or a doer? Are you a go-getter or a grumbler? Are you passionate or procrastinating? Who were you called, created, and destined to be? What is it that you've always dreamed of doing or becoming?

Your answers to these questions are extremely important because greatness can only be defined by you. Greatness cannot be defined by taking the less imaginative path of defining yourself by the standards of others. There is a unique design to you, and you are capable of doing what's necessary to achieve your own personal great at any time in your life. Greatness lies within your ability to fulfill what I call your life's Power Ps: potential, purpose, and personal calling.

Potential

The dictionary defines potential as the capacity to become or to develop into something in the future[1]. The truth is we all have the innate ability and qualities needed to succeed in living our best life, but many of us will never fulfill the potential that lies within. I believe a big reason many of us never achieve our full potential is because we are constantly comparing ourselves to others. Many people think they must have a dynamic personality like Oprah, be a software inventor like Bill Gates, or have outstanding athleticism like LeBron James to be great. But this is simply not true.

Being great is not about being exceptional or doing extraordinary things. It is not about notoriety or being gifted intellectually. Greatness is living and performing in alignment with your own personal "best" in life. It is the process of envisioning the best version of yourself, and then working to be just that - the best *you* that you can be.

You have the capacity to become the greatest version of yourself. This often means forsaking what's good for what's better and what's better for what's best. Reaching your full potential requires you to make choices that may at times be uncomfortable and unpopular with others. But making decisions and stepping out of your comfort zone are critical to achieving your full potential.

Being the very *best you* requires focus, and dare I say, a single-minded focus. This can be a real struggle because having a single-minded focus requires you to decide (1) what is most important to you and (2) how deep you are willing to go to tap into your full potential. Putting your time, attention, and efforts into a single area can create extraordinary results, but it's not easy. Just look at George Washington Carver whose focused research over an eight-year period led to the discovery of more than 300 uses for the peanut. Discoveries that would not have been possible had he not gone deeper in his exploration of the potential of the legume.

> **TRAGEDY IS THE DIFFERENCE BETWEEN WHAT IS AND WHAT COULD HAVE BEEN.**
>
> Abba Eban

There is nothing as tragic as seeing a person with unfulfilled potential. No one wants to be remembered as a "could have been." Unfortunately, we've all known, seen in the media, or read in history books, someone who was seemingly destined for greatness but never achieved it. Consider, for example, athletes who were high draft picks in their respective sport, filled with promise and ability, but who, for a variety of reasons, failed to live up to their full potential.

One such athlete was Bo Jackson. Bo was the first athlete, in the modern era, to possess the power, speed, and skills to play baseball and football in the same year. In 1985 he won the Heisman Trophy and was the number one NFL draft pick. He also played professional baseball with the Kansas City Royals. For three years, he played both sports so well that Nike paid him to advertise their cross-training shoes in a campaign called "Bo Knows." The unfortunate reality was his baseball commitment cut into his football career and vice versa. What's worse, he suffered a hip injury that ended his NFL career after just four seasons. While he continued to play baseball for three more seasons, he played his last game at the age of 31, which is relatively young for a professional athlete.

I want you to consider, for a moment, what Bo Jackson's legacy could have been had he concentrated his efforts, enthusiasm, and energy on maximizing his potential in a single sport. Could it be that his divided focus cost him two careers? In fact, research suggests that people who try to accomplish multiple goals are less committed and less likely to succeed than those who focus on a single goal.[2]

Many of us can probably attest to the difficulty of succeeding when your efforts are split. I am a living testimony to this statement.

When I began writing this book, I was also expanding my coaching and professional development training business, working full-time, and leading the education and marriage ministries, with my husband, at our church. As a result, I lost the energy and focus I needed to finish this project within the time frame I had set for myself.

To get back on track, I needed to ask myself some hard questions. Did the activities and busyness of life contribute to me finishing the book? What was my intent and motive for writing it in the first place? Was the book a simple journal of my thoughts, or did I feel compelled to write it to empower others? Only I could answer these questions and so must you.

While you may be gifted and talented to do many things and have great skills and the capacity to make them happen, the truth is, you must give sustained effort and focus to the thing that will help you to become the best version of you. If you find your attention and focus divided, consider what is truly important in this season. Ask yourself some simple questions. What dream requires your focus to bring it to fruition sooner rather than later? What is it that you feel you are meant to accomplish? What do you need to forsake, forget, or forgo to really forge ahead?

As I mentioned, I believe a huge reason people don't reach their potential is comparison, but more than comparison, is a 4-

> **FEAR IS POWERFUL ENOUGH TO KEEP US FROM ACHIEVING OUR GOALS AND LIVING OUR BEST LIVES.**
>
> Monica Berg

letter word. **F-E-A-R** is the reason that countless people live every day with the capacity to achieve greatness, yet never actualize it. In truth, they have all the necessary abilities and qualities to be successful but never develop them. We have all heard or said statements like, "What if…." or "I don't think I can do it" or "I'm afraid of what others will think". These F-E-A-R statements can be paralyzing. I want you to consider for a moment what purpose fear has served in your life. What opportunities has it kept you from pursuing? What relationships? What adventures?

I have found that fear shows up in several ways and prevents people from fulfilling their potential. For some, it is the fear of the unknown or fear of failure that keeps them from growing and striving for more. For others, it is the fear of inadequacy or of not being enough that has kept them from seeking opportunities. While for still others, it is the fear of rejection or of being judged that has kept them from the potential of having meaningful relationships.

As a person wired for greatness, you must learn to conquer your fears, or at the very least, recognize the fear and continue to push forward. The key to overcoming your fears is to identify them, recognize the excuses you make for yourself, and then focus on positive ways to empower your inner strength. Working through your fear is possible by challenging your thoughts to get to the root of what's causing it.

What fear(s) do you have?

_____

_____

_____

Now consider why you have that fear. For example, a fear of failure could stem from the fact that you saw your parents' life-long dream of running their own business fail.

What could be causing you to have this fear?

_____

_____

_____

_____

What is the worst that can happen if your fear(s) were true?

_____

_____

_____

_____

It is okay to feel fear! The key is acknowledging and facing it, because the truth is, we all have shortcomings. It is your life experiences, the good, the bad, and the ugly that will serve as a point of identification to the people that will be impacted and inspired by you when you fulfill your potential.

Do not let fear box you into a less fulfilling life. Make the decision not to give into your excuses. Take time to honestly examine the possible cause(s) of your fear(s) and allow yourself to experience the emotions associated with them. If necessary, talk it through with a coach or counselor in order to confidently move forward. These steps can help you see your fear as an opportunity rather than an obstacle.

I believe the final reason potential goes unfulfilled is due to complacency. Complacency is a state of ease and contentment typically rooted in comfort with

> THE TRAGEDY OF LIFE IS NOT FOUND IN FAILURE BUT COMPLACENCY. NOT IN YOU DOING TOO MUCH BUT DOING TOO LITTLE. NOT IN LIVING ABOVE YOUR MEANS BUT BELOW YOUR CAPACITY.
>
> Benjamin E. Mays

what has been accomplished thus far. Regardless of having attained certain levels of success, you cannot rely on past achievements to get you to your great. While there is nothing wrong with being content, complacency can prevent you from reaching your full potential by robbing you of ambition and initiative.

Listen to me clearly, regardless of how successful you currently are, there is NO limit to your potential. You can continue to grow and change your entire life. Potential is realized by striving to become all that you are meant to be. You are only limited by your willingness to work hard, dig deep, learn, and develop. Remember greatness is about fulfilling your own potential, purpose, and personal calling. It is measured by your capacity to do, to be, and to become.

You may have convinced yourself that you are the best you can be, while in truth it is possible that you could be even better. I imagine that for many, you are aware that you have the potential to be more, but you are settling because it's easier. While striving to be better does not mean that you will always succeed, to fail means that you have at least tried and have not sat on the sideline wishing, hoping, or resting on your laurels.

For others, I believe you are feeling restless, have a sense of something greater, or just may be wondering "what's my next?" I believe there is untapped potential calling to you. You are feeling this way because you have not yet become all you are meant to be. My advice is, don't settle, don't get stuck in complacency, and don't live below your capacity. You were meant for greatness.

Purpose

> DEEP IN OUR HEARTS, WE ALL WANT TO FIND AND FULFILL A PURPOSE HIGHER THAN OURSELVES. ONLY SUCH A LARGER PURPOSE CAN INSPIRE US TO HEIGHTS THAT WE KNOW WE COULD NEVER REACH ON OUR OWN. FOR EACH OF US THE REAL PURPOSE IS PERSONAL AND PASSIONATE: TO KNOW WHAT WE ARE HERE TO DO, AND WHY.
>
> Os Guiness

Mark Twain famously said, *"The two most important days in your life are the day you are born and the day you find out why"*. As humans, we all share the desire to understand why we exist and what we should be doing. I believe, we each have a unique purpose that answers the question, "Why am I here?" I also recognize that you may be one of the many people who struggle with knowing their purpose. If you have no idea of your "why" at this moment, it is vitally important that you discover it.

It is the discovery of your purpose that reveals your reason for being alive, in this moment, in time, and in this place. Without a sense of purpose people become disillusioned, distracted, and despondent. Look at the statistics on the rates of drug and alcohol abuse, depression, and reliance on antidepressant and anxiety medications that, I believe, point to the crisis of not knowing your purpose. This makes knowing your *why* an important step in becoming the highest and best version of yourself.

Knowing and living in purpose is what gives your life importance and meaning.

Awareness of your purpose means you know your direction. Purpose guides your decisions and goals and points you towards your ultimate destination. Like a navigator using a compass, your purpose is your true north, the point of reference by which all other things are measured. That clarity allows you to concentrate your effort and energy on things that are important to achieving your *great* and to disregard distractions that can derail you.

Purpose powerfully influences your actions, thoughts, and behaviors. By knowing your purpose, you can easily find your fit and gain fulfillment. It enables you to recognize opportunities that are meaningful and rewarding. Knowing your purpose also gives you clarity about your boundaries and knowing what doesn't align with your goals.

Purpose propels and keeps you moving forward even when things around you are difficult and discouraging. A strong purpose is

> HE WHO HAS A WHY CAN ENDURE ANY HOW.
>
> Frederick Nietzsche

critical in developing persistence that resounds across time, trials, and troubles. It provides the resilience needed to overcome any obstacle and challenge that arises on your journey to *great*.

If you are feeling unfulfilled, overwhelmed, and restless, it is because you most likely don't have a clear understanding of your "why". You are out of alignment with your unique purpose, and it is causing you some angst. You are caught between the tension of knowing that who or where you currently are, is not who or where you are destined to be. You may feel stuck in limbo because of that realization.

So, how do you get started identifying your purpose? I believe the answer to that question lies between your perception of *what is* vs. *what could be*. Purpose is the thing that you find meaning in. It is an organic part of who you are. It is the thing that if you did not do it, say it, pursue it, or live it, there would be a void in your life.

I encourage you to follow your curiosity about who you are and the way you are wired. Begin by considering your patterns of thoughts, feelings, and behaviors. Carefully consider these to help you gain some understanding of your "why". I believe that careful consideration of your thoughts, feelings, and behaviors will provide insight into how or what you are uniquely shaped to do, to be, or to become. Don't rush this process. Identifying your purpose is about self-discovery and self-awareness. So, take the time you need to discover your *why* because it is an invaluable part of achieving personal greatness.

What do you often think about or gets you excited?

_____

_____

What is it that you are really concerned about on an emotional and/or spiritual level?

_____

_____

_____

_____

What is the thing that pulls on you, concerns you, and compels you to act?

_____

_____

_____

_____

Considering these three questions collectively, begin crafting your purpose statement. Here's mine, *"My purpose is to inspire and empower others to believe in better so they can achieve personally, meaningful success in their lives."*

_____

_____

_____

_____

Personal Calling

> YOUR CALLING IS WHERE YOUR OWN GREATEST JOY INTERSECTS WITH THE NEEDS OF THE WORLD.
>
> Frederick Buechner

Your purpose and personal calling are inter-connected, but they are not the same. Purpose answers the question, "Why am I here?", while your personal calling is more specific. Think of purpose as the destination and your personal calling as the journey or road taken to get there. In other words, your personal calling is the course of action or path you take to achieve your purpose, and it is lived out through your life and work.

Your personal calling is the area in which you find meaning and have a strong inclination to make an impact on the lives of others. When you operate in your personal calling, you have a sense of what I call "rightness of fit." You know within your being that it is what you were meant to do and where you were meant to be. You will have energy, engagement, and enthusiasm about your personal calling that transcends what may seem like "work" to others. You will feel rewarded in your efforts regardless of whether you receive accolades or recognition for doing it.

Your personal calling serves as the plumb line by which you can measure yourself while in pursuit of fulfilling your unique purpose. When you are following your personal calling, you will feel aligned with your values, motivations, passions, and strengths. You will have a sense of meaning, and a keen awareness of how your actions affect the lives of others. In your personal calling, you feel productive, impactful, and influential. Those who operate in their personal calling generally have greater life satisfaction.

Your personal calling is typically solution oriented and meets the need of something or someone. However, I would caution you not to get locked into a single way of thinking, a single vocation, or a single opportunity. Your personal calling can take the form of different assignments in various stages of your life. In his book Disruptive Thinking, TD Jakes said that you should go beyond identifying your personal calling as just something that you can authentically do because where you begin may not be where you end[2]. This means your initial point of entry into a particular profession or opportunity is only a means of access. Once you have entered, it becomes a place of discovery. Behind each opening you will often find doors, attached to doors, and opportunities attached to opportunities; all of which may align with your values, motivations, passions, and strengths.

> WE ARE NOT IN A POSITION IN WHICH WE HAVE NOTHING TO WORK WITH. WE ALREADY HAVE CAPABILITIES, TALENTS, DIRECTION, MISSIONS, CALLINGS.
>
> Abraham Maslow

When you truly grasp the power of your potential, purpose, and personal calling you will live intentionally to accomplish the greatness that echoes within you. They become the driving forces behind your thoughts and actions and propel you towards the *"you"* that you are meant to be. Your greatness will show up in your confidence and your decision making. You will no longer seek external validation because achieving your personal great is about being authentically who you were created to be. You will make choices that are in alignment with bringing you closer to fulfilling your life's power Ps.

Chapter 2

Excellence

"Excellence is never an accident; it is always the result of high intention, sincere effort, intelligent direction, skillful execution and the vision to see obstacles as opportunities."

- Aristotle

Your journey is not about others. It is not a competition or a race to be won. Your journey is about maximizing your potential and realizing the greatness that lies within. Wherever you are in your life's journey, achieving greatness requires a commitment to becoming your highest and best self. This looks and feels different for each of us. I believe there are four keys that lead to greater levels of personal excellence - clear intention, intelligent direction, sincere action, and skillful execution.

Clear Intention

By default, many people are living out someone else's agenda because they don't have clarity about their own purpose or intentions. Not having clear and focused intentions is another reason people are not living and operating to their full potential. Living with intention means that you are actively engaged in creating the life you want and the person you want to become. You can only live intentionally to the extent to which you have clarity around your power "P"s.

A lack of clarity can lead to you engaging in actions and efforts that don't produce the results you want for your life. This can lead to you becoming internally frustrated and cause you to look outward to others and pursue their ideals of your purpose. This can ultimately lead to a lack of contentment and dissatisfaction because your unique purpose is always personal and passionate. Therefore, it is necessary that you gain clarity around who you are, what you desire in life, and what you want to achieve. Clarity of intention sharpens your awareness of what is truly valuable and empowers you to steward your time and energy wisely.

Intelligent Direction

Having clarity about your intention allows you to answer the question, *"Is this in alignment with who I see myself becoming?"*. On the path to success, you will encounter distractions and detractors that will attempt to stand in opposition to your achievement of greatness. You must develop your abilities to recognize, understand, and effectively handle the problems and the people that will attempt to disrupt your progress. Developing these abilities will help you navigate in an intelligent direction.

To move in an intelligent direction is to purposefully manage your actions so that they align with the attainment of your Power Ps. You must be mindful and not yield to instinctive, emotional actions or responses that can be detrimental to your progress. Rather, make a conscious decision to engage in actions that move you towards greatness.

You must learn to operate in a manner that is thoughtful and deliberate and keeps you focused on your "why". Your purpose is the purest source of direction in achieving your personal greatness. Following your purpose is the best indication of whether you are moving along the correct path. Knowing and remembering your "why" keeps you focused and pointed toward your true north.

Sincere Effort

Without a sincere effort all your dreams and goals are of no value. The unfortunate thing is that most people will put in the work needed for a short time but soon give up when their desired outcomes are not immediate. Sincere effort isn't something you only do once. It must be applied consistently and speaks to your belief in yourself, goals, and dreams. When you are willing to apply the sincere effort to do what is necessary it is a demonstration that you believe what you are doing is valuable. As a result, your consistent efforts, pointed in an intelligent direction, progressively moves you closer and closer to achieving success.

Execution

Excellence embodies the skillful execution of your intended goals and objectives. This requires you to take time to be clear and methodical about what you want to accomplish. In other words, you need to create a plan. You must get organized before you take action. Initially, this involves identifying the "what" of your *why*. What is the big picture or long-term goal? What are the resources that you will need? What barriers do you anticipate? What does success look like for you?

Next you must determine your "who". Although you may have intrinsic talents, skills, and intelligence, no man is an island, and greatness cannot be achieved alone. True success requires the collaboration of others. You need pivotal people on your journey who will come alongside to support, encourage, and advise you. These key people are the ones who will hold you accountable for achieving your goals.

After you have considered the "what" and "who", you then must consider the "how" to best achieve your goal. The "how" involves the steps and behaviors that you must execute in order to achieve excellence. Whatever your how, it will require discipline. This is where a lot of people falter. People with great intentions become distracted from their goals because they don't exercise the needed discipline.

> SELF-DISCIPLINE BEGINS WITH THE MASTERY OF YOUR THOUGHTS. IF YOU DON'T CONTROL WHAT YOU THINK, YOU CAN'T CONTROL WHAT YOU DO.
>
> Unknown

Discipline is extremely important because it provides direction, structure, and time management. It is the ability to remain determined, committed, and focused even in the face of adversity. The first step to exercising discipline is to identify and engage in the thinking and behaviors you need to be successful. For some, it may mean changing the course of your education, your career path, or your habits. For others, it may mean abandoning something you are currently doing to do something completely different. You must identify the habits and ways of thinking that you must start, stop, or continue to achieve your personal best.

The call to greatness begins with excellence. But it doesn't happen overnight. Legendary coach John Wooden said, *"It takes time to create excellence. If it could be done quickly, more people would do it."* Seek to do well in all your endeavors, and don't settle for less than what you can achieve. When you fall short of your goals, recast your vision, reset your focus, and strive to do better the next time. Remember, what matters most is that *you* become the person you are meant to be.

What disciplined thinking and/or behavior(s) must you start, stop, or continue to operate in excellence?

_____

_____

_____

_____

_____

Chapter 3

Consistency

"Motivation gets you going, but discipline keeps you growing. That's the Law of Consistency. It doesn't matter how talented you are. It doesn't matter how many opportunities you receive. If you want to grow, consistency is key."

- John C. Maxwell

Consistency is often the difference between success and failure. The problem with understanding the importance of consistency in achieving greatness is that most people tend to confuse consistency with routine. Routine is a sequence of actions that one regularly follows, or a repeated way of doing things in a specific manner or order.

Routines are significant and ensure that you are persistent in doing the things that are important. A great example of following a routine is my husband Kennen, who is a natural bodybuilder. He has a routine of rising early, doing strength and conditioning exercises, and eating a specific diet regime. While training for a competition, he does this daily, week in and week out. What separates him from others, who he competes against, is his consistency in adherence to the same routine.

Consistency

Consistency takes routine further in the sense that one's actions and attitudes are without contradiction, even in less than convenient or unfavorable times. For instance, Kennen has often been 'in training' during vacations, family reunions, and anniversary celebrations. Where others might skip a day at the gym or cheat on their diets during these occasions, his motto is, *"I don't train for second place. While I'm taking a day off, the competition isn't"*.

Kennen's dedication and commitment to consistently engage in a set of routine behaviors, have brought him repeated success. He adheres to the same set of principle ways of behaving and believing during his training periods. Year after year, he has kept his body in a physical condition that most people his age envy. Most don't believe that he is technically a senior citizen, and you certainly wouldn't know it just by looking at him. In his bodybuilding career, he has won a total of 49 times with only 2 second place finishes. At the time of this writing, he had won his most recent competition at the tender age of 61 years old!

> TO GET THE RESULTS YOU WANT, YOU DON'T HAVE TO BE EXTREME, JUST CONSISTENT.
>
> Anonymous

Achieving greatness requires dedication and repeatedly doing what's necessary to achieve a goal. Successful people do consistently what unsuccessful people do occasionally. While consistency and routine do lead to success, it doesn't mean that every day will be easy or without hiccups. Consistency also doesn't mean sticking to what's not working for the sake of consistency. Sometimes your routine needs to change. Success comes from constantly engaging in routines that are working, sticking to them until they don't, and adjusting practices until you find what works again.

The key to consistency is having a defined set of 'always' behaviors. These are the actions and attitudes that are repeatedly employed and create momentum that moves you in the direction of greatness. Your always behaviors are invaluable and are the standard by which you operate in fulfillment of your Power Ps. They serve as a reminder and as an opportunity to be consistent in those things that increase the likelihood of your success.

For some, an 'always' behavior might look like daily reading blogs or listening to podcasts in your area of business. For others, it might look like going for a daily 5-mile run or eating a healthy diet to reach or maintain your desired weight. For still others, it may be setting aside an hour a day to meditate and pray to grow spiritually. Your 'always' behaviors will be unique to you and based on your potential, purpose, and personal calling. The more consistent you are in engaging in the key behaviors that will unlock your personal great, the greater the likelihood of achieving it.

Consistency

What are at least two 'always' behaviors that you must do consistently to propel you toward success?

_____

_____

_____

_____

> CONSISTENCY IS THE BELT THAT FASTENS EXCELLENCE IN POSITION. IF YOU DON'T DO IT REPEATEDLY, YOU'LL NOT EXCEL IN IT.
>
> Israelmore Ayivor

Chapter 4

Hustle

"Things may come to those who wait, but only the things left by those who hustle."

- Abraham Lincoln

To achieve greatness requires a hustle mentality. To hustle is to do what is necessary, for as long as is necessary, to achieve your personal great. It is the mental attitude, with corresponding actions, that enthusiastically pursues becoming all that you are meant to be. Having a hustle mentality means going after what you want, rather than sitting and waiting for permission. It is the awareness that the pursuit of greatness doesn't require you to follow the way that it's always been done or to wait your turn. It's a mindset that helps you to discover your own way forward when there is no well-traveled path. Hustle is a way of thinking that fully owns the idea that you can accomplish your dream even when doors are seemingly closed. It's the attitude of persistence in the face of obstacles.

> HOLD YOURSELF RESPONSIBLE FOR A HIGHER STANDARD THAN ANYBODY ELSE EXPECTS OF YOU. NEVER EXCUSE YOURSELF. NEVER PITY YOURSELF...
>
> Henry Ward Beecher

Hustle

I really identify with the quote I referenced by Henry Beecher because like me, you may have had setbacks in life that placed you in a seemingly disadvantaged position. You may not have the innate ability, talents, or winning personality that others have, or you may not have been born with certain economic privileges. However, you cannot use that as an excuse to not strive for the greatness that lives within. What you have or don't have, what has happened to you in the past, really has no bearing on your future. Your past and/or present circumstances are not the reason you can't succeed, they are the conditions and experiences from which you must succeed. In essence, they are what propel you towards the greatness within.

Your full potential lies underneath all the *haves*. The *would haves…I would have gone to college, if….*; the *could haves…I could have been so much farther in my career, if….*; the *should haves…I should have done this when….* Then there are the maybes *of life…. Maybe if someone gave me a chance; maybe if I was born into wealth*, etc., etc., etc. Beloved, hear my heart on this. Get over yourself!

I'm not saying that you don't have valid reasons for why you are, where you are. But they are not an excuse for settling for less than being the best that you can be. Never pity yourself. Self-pity drains your energy and pulls you into a spiral of negativity. While there is value in the acknowledgement of painful experiences, don't get stuck there. Take responsibility for the parts of your life that you can change and hold yourself to an expectation of greater. Control the controllable; and you can only control *you*. You alone are responsible for your attitude, your hustle, and your achievements.

Hustle requires a "right now" attitude. You must possess a sense of urgency because time is precious. You must have a mindset that constantly strives to fulfill your Power Ps and takes the initiative to make them a reality. Greatness requires work. You cannot do the bare minimum, coast along, and think that everything will magically fall into place. Just showing up is not enough. Making excuses for why you "can't" won't cut it. You can either make excuses, or you can make progress. It's your choice!

> YOU CAN'T CHEAT THE GRIND; IT KNOWS HOW MUCH YOU HAVE INVESTED. IT WON'T GIVE YOU ANYTHING YOU HAVEN'T WORKED FOR.
>
> Unknown

There are no short cuts to becoming your ideal self. You must be willing to do the hard, but necessary work to achieve success. You must do the things that average people are not willing to do. It requires you to learn what is needed to achieve greatness and work hard to accomplish it. You can fulfill your Power Ps through discipline, hustle, doing what needs to be done, and never giving up. Only you know how many late nights, sacrifices, and amount of work you must put in to achieve your own personal greatness.

Even though there is no timetable for success, you must not waste time pursuing things that don't matter. Design your life around what it will take to achieve your personal great and engage in opportunities every day that will make it happen. We will discuss the importance of identifying, discerning, and taking advantage of opportunities in the next chapter. But I want to caution you that when you operate with a hustle mentality, opportunities will present themselves. However they may not be consistent with your purpose or personal calling. Don't allow distractions to derail you.

Just because you *can* do something, doesn't mean that you *should*. Avoid the temptation to go in different directions. Stay focused and recognize what you should give your attention to and what you should ignore. In a world with so many interruptions, this takes intentionality.

A last word about hustle. Understand, I'm not advocating working intensively or with a grind that doesn't allow for a work/life balance. While there are things you will have to sacrifice on your journey to success - your health, family, mental, and personal well-being should not be on that altar. Hustle is not about overworking to the point of exhaustion, but it is about developing and executing the high impact habits, which position you for success.

Chapter 5

Opportunity

The golden opportunity you are seeking is within yourself.

- Mary Engelbreit

I often hear people say things like, *"If I just had the opportunity, then…."* or *"If someone would give me a chance, I would…."* Those statements sound reasonable when you consider the definition of opportunity which is a set of circumstances that make it possible to do something.[1] However, I question, why must you wait for others to give you an opportunity?

It is my earnest belief that you attract opportunities just by fulfilling your potential, purpose, and personal calling.

When you have discovered and function within your Power Ps you won't have to wait for others to give you a favorable set of circumstances. Opportunities will come to you. The challenge is learning to recognize your moments of opportunities. Many people miss their moments because opportunities present themselves in the most unexpected ways. Opportunities surround us every day and here's the secret to recognizing them...are you ready for it? Opportunities often come disguised as problems. That's right, as problems.

Opportunity

Every problem has a solution, and I believe you were born to solve some problem on this earth. Your *why* is the answer to an issue, dilemma, or crisis in your family, community, organization, etc. When you encounter problems and obstacles, seek to be solution oriented. Learn to trust your instincts and listen to your inner voice to embrace new ideas and possibilities to solve the problems or challenges that you encounter.

Problems solvers are influencers. Your influence will increase in direct proportion to your ability to solve problems. The more problems you solve, the more influence you gain. The more influence you gain, the more opportunity comes to you. That's more opportunity to impact people, systems, and ways of thinking for the betterment of others.

Many have seized the opportunity to harness the power of Facebook, Instagram, Tik Tok, YouTube, and the like to become major influencers of current culture. Although I don't believe this is necessarily a bad thing, I would caution that achieving personal greatness is not about pop culture fads, fashions, or phenoms. Maximizing opportunity is using your influence and impact for significance, not just success. Your personal great is the pursuit of the purpose for which you were created, not the quest for likes, looks, or loot.

An essential aspect of achieving greatness involves opening yourself up to different possibilities and paths that may lead to the fulfillment of your personal best. Becoming skilled at seeing opportunities and using them as catalysts to propel you toward your intended end takes time to develop. Don't limit yourself to what you already know. Explore options beyond the familiar. This requires embracing experiences that are outside your comfort zone. When you are not open to different experiences, it limits your view of what's possible and limits your potential.

> GREAT OPPORTUNITIES MAY COME ONCE IN A LIFETIME, BUT SMALL OPPORTUNITIES SURROUND US EVERY DAY.
>
> Rick Warren

Take the opportunity to delve into diverse activities, develop new relationships with people, and discover non-traditional ways of thinking. Be curious and be open to change. Spend time devouring information, asking questions, and honing your craft. If there are new concepts, innovations, and ways of doing things around your purpose and personal calling, make it your business to know what they are.

Explore opportunities that are in alignment with where you are going. Take advantage of opportunities and proactively pursue them. Manage the opportunities you receive effectively, putting in the sincere effort to guarantee that they are maximized. This will require you to discern whether the timing is

Opportunity

right, and you are ready to handle everything that comes with the opportunity.

As much as you might want to embrace a particular opportunity, you must be honest with yourself and be okay declining it. Don't make the mistake of mishandling an opportunity because you aren't ready for it. The urgency of the hustle discussed in the previous chapter must be tempered with adequate preparation. You can have the skillset, but not the maturity to deal with everything that comes with opportunity.[2] Therefore, understanding your readiness, or lack thereof, for an opportunity requires a healthy dose of self-awareness.

What problem exists that you believe you have the answer to?

_____

_____

_____

What experiences, activities, or people must you engage with to attract opportunities that are in alignment with your purpose or personal calling?

_____

_____

_____

_____

Chapter 6

Pivotal People

"You have to believe it's possible and believe in yourself. Because after you've decided what you want, you have to believe it's possible, and possible for you, not just for other people. Then you need to seek out models, mentors, and coaches."

- Jack Canfield

To achieve true greatness requires pivotal people that help you along the way. These are individuals who serve as role models, mentors, coaches, or sponsors at different points in your journey. Understanding their unique role, and knowing which pivotal person is required, in a particular stage of your life can provide valuable insight into propelling you toward the accomplishment of your goals. Often, the personal and professional skills, knowledge, and expertise you need to be successful will dictate which pivotal person is needed. In one season, you may need help achieving a higher level of performance. In another, you may need accountability for achieving a specific goal. In another, you may need a person who introduces you to others in a particular business area. Let's take a brief look at each pivotal person.

Role Model

A role model is someone who has traits you admire and wish to emulate. You may never meet this person but admire certain skills that they have. For instance, I wish to be able to inspire others the way Lisa Nichols inspires others to give their dreams a chance. I've never met Lisa, but that doesn't stop me from respecting and admiring her unique ability to be authentic to herself and her audience.

> BEING A ROLE MODEL IS NOT JUST ABOUT WHAT YOU DO; IT'S ABOUT WHAT YOU INSPIRE OTHERS TO BECOME.
>
> Aaron Kroon

Role models are important because they provide motivation, inspiration, and, if you are in relationship with them, support. These are individuals that you look to as a template for success. They model the behaviors and habits that inspire you to become better. However, I must caution you, be sure to select role models that have the same values, beliefs, and principles as you do. This is important because our culture is highly influenced by social media. We all have been exposed to individuals whom I call anti-role models. Their unethical character and just plain bad behavior has caused many to lose sight of their own moral compass. If you need a role model, consider people who you admire and whose life, core values, and integrity match your own.

Coach

A coach is someone who works with you and provides guidance as you try to perfect a skill. Coaching is short-term and aimed at addressing areas identified by you. Coaching is focused on supporting your personal and professional growth based on a self-initiated change. This is most often in pursuit of reaching your own objectives for personal or professional success. The coach's role is to help you explore issues, unblock barriers, see

> COACHING HELPS YOU TAKE STOCK OF WHERE YOU ARE NOW IN ALL ASPECTS OF LIFE.
>
> Elaine McDonald

different perspectives, and increase the options that are available to you.[2]

Your coach will consider your past performance and events, but they will also focus on actions and goals for the future. Their approach is action oriented, focusing on where you are now, where you want to be in the future, and how best to get you there. Based on your needs, there are several categories of coaches to help you reach your highest and best self. Some great examples of coaching support include life coaches, relationship coaches, business coaches, and high-performance coaches. To establish a coaching relationship, begin by asking others for recommendations or referrals. Investigate Google reviews and other websites for testimonials, browse professional membership directories, or attend networking events and conferences.

Mentor

A mentor is someone who talks with you about your career, goals, plans, and aspirations. The aim of mentoring is to provide you with the needed support that will enable you to move forward confidently and to achieve your objective(s). Mentoring generally takes the form of a confidential, one-to-one relationship. The mentor offers supportive and non-threatening guidance and advice. He or she helps you refine your plans, suggest people you should talk to, recommend opportunities you should partake in, and recognize obstacles you should be aware of.

> A MENTOR IS SOMEONE WHO SEES MORE TALENT AND ABILITY WITHIN YOU THAN YOU SEE IN YOURSELF AND HELPS BRING IT OUT OF YOU.
>
> Bob Proctor

Mentors usually take on the role of motivating and inspiring you towards your next milestone or goal. Mentorship is a long-term relationship, often continuing for years or a lifetime. Therefore, it is very important that the mentor you select is a person who has enthusiasm and a passion for helping others to develop, fulfill their potential, and achieve their objectives. If you need a mentor, first reach out to see if they would be willing to connect with you and give you some advice. Come prepared with a few questions on a specific topic and ask if you can follow up after you've implemented their advice. While a mentor is someone who can give you advice to help you navigate tricky or sticky situations, they don't necessarily have the power or authority to intervene directly on your behalf.

Sponsor

Whereas mentors are people who talk *with* you, sponsors are people who talk *about* you when you're not in the room. They are the people who endorse and champion you from behind closed doors. Sponsors take what they know about you, what you want to become, and where you want to go and advocate for you. They use their power, resources, and influence to push for you. They nominate you for committees, opportunities, awards, and promotions. They typically have gained connections both professionally and personally, and they're willing to use their influence to open doors that might otherwise be closed to you.

I've had such people in my life and career and can assure you that sponsors are extremely beneficial. The most important thing that I would share in securing the support of someone who vocally advocates for you is to gain a good reputation. Work hard so that others notice. Demonstrate your value and follow through with commitments to build trust. You want to have a reputation for the right reasons because the person who sponsors you will be risking their reputation on yours. Sponsor relationships typically happen organically because that person has spent time observing you and feels confident speaking up on your behalf. If a sponsor is needed, remember to let your work and behavior speak for themselves. Gain a reputation for excellence.

It's important to identify pivotal people that will challenge you to be the highest version of yourself. In doing so, the benefits can be great and can help you to avoid mistakes in your personal or professional life, achieve more in less time, minimize problems, and effectively prepare for potential difficulties. I have personally found that having pivotal people in my life at strategic times has assisted me in decisions to change career direction, becoming more influential in business, and being more empathetic in personal areas. They helped me to identify blind spots and empowered me to make the sometimes hard but necessary changes that have thrusted my life and my career forward.

To benefit from a pivotal person in your life requires you to be coachable and teachable. This is an indication that you are open to becoming a better you. Even though you may be a professional in your respective field or at the top of your game in your industry, it is important to have humility, self-awareness, and a willingness to learn from others.

Pivotal People

Deliberately select people who challenge and drive you to higher levels. Don't allow age or position to be a deterrent in gleaning from a person's knowledge and experience. Recognizing pivotal people at the right time can help you to overcome challenges and excel in life and your career.

> SPONSORSHIP ABOUT PUTTING YOUR NAME AND REPUTATION ON THE LINE FOR SOMEONE ELSE. IT COULD BE AS SIMPLE AS RECOMMENDING SOMEONE FOR A NEW ROLE, YET IT'S ONE OF THE MOST POWERFUL CULTURAL TOOLS AN ORGANIZATION HAS.
>
> Lynne Doughtie

Consider which of the following is most pivotal for you on this leg of your journey.

☐ role model

☐ coach

☐ mentor

☐ sponsor

Once you have identified the type of person that is most pivotal, take time to consider how you can select, contact, and/or hire that person.

Chapter 7

Your Life's Blueprint

"When you live with intentionality, you know and understand that every day is your time to make a difference".

- Steve Gutzler

In 2016, God gave me a vision for a business called Blueprint4Change. At that time, I had a different idea of what I thought was the purpose for the business. For many years, I let the concept lie dormant until I gained clarity around its actual purpose. It wasn't until seven years later that I had enough knowledge, exposure, and preparation, and was adequately positioned to accomplish the intended purpose of what the business was meant to be.

The vision behind Blueprint4Change is to empower others to become people of confidence, competence, and influence through coaching and professional development training. A significant core of the business is helping people to define and align with their potential, purpose, and personal calling. This alignment begins with creating a blueprint for the goals and actions they will take that empowers them to lean into their call to greatness.

How you see yourself is the most important step in defining your blueprint for life. As Dr. Martin Luther King, Jr. said, you must have *"a deep belief in your own dignity, your own worth, and your own somebodiness"*.[1] You must believe that your life has value. You were born for and with a unique purpose which means your life has significance. Therefore, take pride in who you are. Maintain self-respect, behave with dignity, and honor your own individuality. Have confidence in the fact that you are worthy of all that will come to you as you respond to the echo of greatness.

Second, you must have *"the determination to achieve excellence in your various fields of endeavor."*[2] Your life's purpose will be accomplished as you operate in your personal calling. Whatever you set out to, do it wholeheartedly, and do it well. Whether or not you know your specific calling at this time, understand that everyone is good at something, and you add value to others by doing it. When you discover your "something", you can make an extraordinary impact on the life of others by simply striving to be the best that you can be. In fact, when you excel at being you, your life just may become the blueprint for others to follow. It is my belief that you can create an enduring legacy for generations to come, that speaks to how ordinary people can have extraordinary impact just by living out their purpose and personal calling.

Your Life's Blueprint

Like a custom home design, the blueprint for your life is a detailed view of what greatness looks like for you. Your blueprint will be executed through the fulfillment of your potential, purpose, and personal calling. This means you are the architect, the construction foreman, and the building inspector. The quality of your finished product will be directly related to how you lean into the ECHO responding with excellence, consistency, hustle, and taking advantage of opportunity.

> **THE BLUEPRINT FOR SUCCESS IS INSIDE OF YOU. IT WILL STAY THERE UNLESS YOU TAKE IT OUT AND CREATE IT.**
>
> Larina Kase

Final Thoughts

"Your greatness is not revealed by the lights that shine on you, but the light that shines within you."

- Ray Davis

Greatness looks different for everyone. I believe that many of you have heard the ECHO of greatness. However, there may be others that didn't know that greatness is even an option. Prior to reading this book, you may have been unaware of the fact that you could become more and had a low ceiling of expectation. You may have been genuinely unaware of the potential you have or that you can even pursue a more meaningful and fulfilling path.

The truth is, if you cannot picture your own greatness, you can never achieve your potential, purpose, or personal calling. Therefore, it is important to have a vision of greatness. While sometimes models exist, those who become great are often trail blazers. What is important is that you see

> A VISION IS NOT JUST A PICTURE OF WHAT COULD BE; IT IS AN APPEAL TO OUR BETTER SELVES, A CALL TO BECOME SOMETHING MORE.
>
> Rosabeth Moss Kanter

something more than the present circumstances in which you find yourself. This begins with asking yourself thought-provoking questions that push you to explore what is possible. The key is to be honest with yourself.

Don't allow complacency and fear to limit you. Be willing to change rather than live with the regret of what could have been. Attack life head on with the intent of giving it everything you have. Prioritize what's important and hustle. Hone your craft, push through obstacles, break down barriers, and leave your mark.

Do everything with the goal of achieving your personal great. Pursue excellence by giving your best effort in all that you do. Take advantage of every opportunity that presents itself that's in alignment with where you are going. When setbacks occur, learn from them, and move forward. Never stop and keep moving on the path to greatness.

> I BELIEVE THAT WE ARE CALLED BY GOD TO BE THE VERY BEST STEWARDS OF ALL THE GIFTS, TALENTS, AND OPPORTUNITIES ENTRUSTED TO US IN THIS LIFETIME. THE RESULT IS TRUE PROSPERITY, REAL SUCCESS.
>
> T.D. Jakes

Understand that achieving greatness is not about you alone. You are called and destined to make an impact in life. Don't rest on your success or sit comfortably on the sidelines while there is still good to be done in this world. Whatever pulls at your heart strings, whatever compels you to speak and act, do it with all of your heart, soul, mind, and strength. Let your true greatness shine through!

Lastly, I recognize that there are a vast number of people searching for something to give their lives meaning, purpose, and direction. There is an inner void that causes many to have a sense of incompleteness. To reiterate, it is the inner voice of your Creator, calling you to something more. As a person of faith in Jesus, the Christ, I would be remiss if I didn't share with you that He can fill that void and reveal to you true purpose. I encourage you to start your journey to personal fulfillment by letting His presence fill you.

You can receive the gift of His presence, simply by inviting Him into your life, acknowledging your need for Him, and believing that He lived, died, and lives again by the power of God. Through Christ you are brought into a relationship with our Creator. He lives to help you, empower you, give you strength and hope so that greatness within you can be revealed.

Notes

The Power Ps

1. "potential." *Merriam-Webster.com* 2024. https://www.merriam-webster.com (15 January 2024).
2. Amy N. Dalton and Stephen A. Spiller (2012). *Too Much of a Good Thing: The Benefits of Implementation Intentions Depend on the Number of Goals.* Journal of Consumer Research
3. TD Jakes. *Disruptive Thinking* (New York: Faith Words, 2023), 29.

Opportunity

1. "opportunity." *Oxfordlearnersdictionaries.com* 2024. https://www.oxfordlearnersdictionaries.com (20 January 2024).

2. Joseph Walker, III. *No Opportunity Wasted: The Art of Execution*. (Nashville: Heritage Publishing, 2017), 23.

Pivotal People

1. International Coach Federation (ICF) (2024)
2. Hayley Stanton. (16 May 2019). *What is coaching? What's the role of a coach?* https://quietconnections.co.uk

Your Life's Blueprint

1. Beacon Press. (19 May 2015). *What's your life's blueprint?* [Video]. YouTube https://www.youtube.com/watch?v=ZmtOGXreTOU&t=1215s

About the Author

Sherri Brooks, PhD is an ICF certified executive and leadership development coach, speaker, and professional development trainer. In her 20+ year career, she has held corporate and executive career roles in operations, academia, clinical, healthcare, and business entrepreneurship. From helping individuals and organizations to identify strengths and needed areas of development to advancing leadership competencies, Dr. Sherri empowers others to identify and engage in actionable strategies that will move them forward in achieving their goals. Her aim is simple: to empower individuals to live and lead with confidence, competence, and influence.

Her ASCEND beyond the expected brand, which stands for **A**rise to **S**ignificance, **C**larity, **E**xcellence, and **N**ecessary **D**isruption, was born from her own personal journey of overcoming adversity, challenges, and barriers. She leverages her expertise and experiences from her humble beginnings as a teen mom, to a successful corporate leader and entrepreneur, to guide others through an intentional process of personal and professional change. She is passionate about inspiring others to rise above their circumstances and achieve their full potential.

She is happily married to Kennen Brooks. Together, they are committed to seeing couples win in relationships and marriage. Through their marriage coaching, they authentically influence and empower couples to have relationships that reflect unity, love, laughter, and intimacy. January 2025, they will launch their H.E.A.RT. podcast to empower couples to have **H**onest **E**xchanges **A**bout **R**elationships & **T**rust. Be sure to tune in and subscribe to YouTube and all your podcast listening platforms.

> DO MORE THAN BELONG:
> PARTICIPATE.
>
> DO MORE THAN CARE:
> HELP.
>
> DO MORE THAN BELIEVE:
> PRACTICE.
>
> — William Arthur Ward

Invitation to Connect

Dr. Sherri would love to hear from you and know how you've been encouraged through her writing, or for more information about her speaking, coaching and leadership development opportunities, contact her at any of the following:

www.drsherribrooks.com

www.blueprint4change.org

https://www.linkedin.com/in/drsherribrooks/

Made in the USA
Columbia, SC
06 February 2025